Living in Big Tujunga Canyon

*She nurtured life with water and woods,
then with angry, thundering waves,
washed it away.*

**The Early History of Sunland, California
Volume 7**

ML Tiernan

Living in Big Tujunga Canyon

www.maryleetiernan.com
Second printing April 1, 2015
10 9 8 7 6 5 4 3 2

ISBN 978-0983067269 (Paperback)

©2001 ©2010 Mary Lee Tiernan. All rights reserved. No portion of this product may be photographed, scanned, translated, reproduced, copied, or reduced to any tangible or electronic medium or machine-readable form, without the prior written consent of Mary Lee Tiernan.

Photograph on the cover courtesy of Bolton Hall Museum, Tujunga, California.
Quote on the cover is from John W. Robinson's *The San Gabriels*, p. 5.

Contents

In the Beginning 5

Early Homesteaders 11

Half a Century Later 25

Footnotes 37

Bibliography 38

The Early History of Sunland, California series 40

Author's Notes

The researcher, like a detective, examines the evidence to try to determine the real story. Unfortunately for researchers, we cannot re-examine witnesses or revisit scenes because in most cases, they have long since disappeared. So we sort through the conflicting data to find the most reliable and logical explanations. I have done my best to follow the clues and weave as authentic a story as possible.

My thanks to the staff at Bolton Hall Museum, Tujunga, California, for their assistance with this project.

In the Beginning...

In days past, Big Tujunga Canyon bristled with life. Grizzly bears roamed through forests of live oak, cottonwood, walnut, alder, and willow trees. Seeds, animals, and birds traveled from the desert in the north through the canyon to the southern slopes. In the wash—a flood plain about a quarter of a mile wide at the base of the canyon—the seeds rooted and thrived, offering a unique blend of brush and wildlife from different climatic zones.

Big Tujunga Canyon and Wash. Photo courtesy of Bruce Perry.

Through it all, the river flowed freely, bringing its life-sustaining nourishment.

The denuding of the canyon began in the early 1800s with the building of the San Fernando Mission, which needed lumber for its construction and grazing land for its large herds of cattle. The padres lost their rights to the mission lands only decades later when the Mexican government, which ruled California, secularized the land in 1833 and redistributed it as land grants.

In 1840, brothers Francisco and Pedro Lopez were given part of the former San Fernando Mission lands to raise cattle. On their Rancho Tujunga, vaqueros herded cattle and horses far into the mouth of Big Tujunga Canyon with its abundant supply of chaparral and water. The discovery of the Lopez documents ended the once-popular belief that the Verdugo family land grant which encompassed parts of Glendale, La Crescenta, and La Canada had also included the Sunland-Tujunga area.

With the ranches and horses came the horse thieves. In the dense woodlands of the canyons, many a bandit hid from the law. The notorious Tiburcio Vasquez used the San Gabriel Mountains as his hideout for more than 20 years. During his last escapade in April 1874, he eluded capture by climbing into the mountains near La Canada, crossing through Vasquez Canyon to the Big Tujunga, then slipping down the Big Tujunga Canyon, or the BT in local parlance, to the valley. Vasquez Canyon's name recalls that last dramatic getaway.

Big Tujunga provided timber for many a long-gone cabin or hacienda. The rapidly growing city of Los Angeles needed wood, lots of wood. To satisfy this hunger for fuel and building materials, woodcutters cut down the oak and pine trees growing in abundance along the fringes of the mountains and in the canyon and then hauled the logs by horse and

Big Tujunga Canyon

wagon down the valley through Glendale. Many of their paths became the early roads in the valley.

While the woodcutters stripped the canyon of trees, hundreds of prospectors flocked to the BT in the 1870s and 1880s after the discovery of gold. They mined the earth for placer gold and the richer gold-bearing quartz until the craze for gold sent them after the next strike. While they plundered the earth beneath the canyon's surface, hunters and fishermen arrived in larger and larger numbers to kill the canyon's wildlife for sport. Bear, mountain lions, and deer, as well as smaller game, fell to the bang of a gun.

The lands surrounding the canyon attracted farmers who tilled the fertile land, rich from soil washed down the mountain. Some like Pedro Ybarra came to farm; some like Farmer Johnson came as woodcutters, but stayed to ranch. Others like Sherman Page and F.C. Howes came to cash in on the land boom and build a town.[1]

And so the white man began to inhabit the lands where the Gabrielino Indians had walked for thousands of years. A branch of the Gabrielinos—the Tuhunga Indians—had settled in the distant past in the region near Hansen Dam. Older documents refer to Lake View Terrace as Tuhunga Valley because of its proximity to the original village of the Tuhungas, not to be confused with the much later city of Tujunga to the east.

The exact meaning of the name Tuhunga is lost in time. For some, it comes from an old Gabrielino word meaning 'place of the old woman,' suggesting a tribute to Mother Earth and to the bounty of the canyon. Some claim the word means 'big thunder,' aptly named for those times when Mother Earth sends boulders and swollen flood waters crashing down the canyon. From the time the Lopez brothers established their rancho, spelling variations of *Tejunga* or *Tujunga* or even *Tijunga* began to appear. The more commonly used *Tujunga* became the accepted spelling.

Whatever the original name meant or the variations in spelling, the duality of the canyon challenged those who chose to live there. They traded enjoyment of its beauty for harsh living conditions—especially from flood waters tearing down the mountainside and washing out roads, leaving them isolated on the mountain. Man may borrow the canyon, but he will never tame her.

Sunland Park in the 1880-1890s

Early Sunland
Photos courtesy of Bolton Hall Museum.

Early Homesteaders

Cornelius and Alice Johnson wound their way over the rough ground, thick with bushes. Their footsteps obliterated those left by the deer on the narrow trail to Big Tujunga Canyon. The afternoon sun warmed their backs on that fall afternoon in 1916[2] as they bent to clear brush from the entrance of the canyon basin. Like the Gabrielino

Villagers took turns posing with the grizzly.
Photo courtesy of Bolton Hall Museum.

Indians who'd lived there for centuries past, the Johnsons knew that clearing the trail kept the canyon passable and helped prevent the spread of forest fires.

Spotting some unusual tracks on the soft ground, Alice called to her husband. Cornelius joined her and bent down to examine the earth. To his surprise, he recognized the imprints as bear tracks. While grizzlies had once freely roamed the canyons, most had disappeared as man settled in. Knowing the grizzly could be vicious, Cornelius took Alice safely home. He grabbed his shotgun and returned to search the area, but did not see the bear.

A few days later, Cornelius found evidence of the bear feeding on the lower section of the ranch. Honey from their beehives and the ripe fruit still hanging on their trees attracted the bear and would keep it in the vicinity. Fearful for his seven-year-old daughter Lucille who walked to school through this section of the ranch, Cornelius set a trap and lashed it to a log.

When Cornelius checked the next morning, both trap and log had disappeared. He tracked the bear by following the thrashed brush all the way up the mountain. Worn out from fighting the log he dragged with him, the bear, still caught in the trap, collapsed when the log jammed between two trees. Without hesitation, Cornelius aimed his 30-30 and shot the bear once behind the ear. Newspapers would later call it the $1,000 shot, claiming the rare silvertip grizzly would have been worth $1,000 or more if taken alive.[3]

News of the kill spread quickly. Neighbors arrived to help chain the 300 pound carcass to a pole and bring it down the mountain to the community's central gathering place, Sunland Park. An unofficial holiday ensued. After everyone finished posing for pictures with the bear, Cornelius skinned the bear late in the evening, and the town feasted on barbecued meat. Loron Rowley sold the remainder of that "awful, racid"[4] meat in his general store. The saga of the last silver-tipped grizzly found in Southern California south of the Tehachapi Mountains ended with Cornelius making a rug out of the hide and head. His daughters eventually donated it to the Museum of Natural History in Exposition Park, Los Angeles.

Years earlier, sixteen-year-old Cornelius[5] had arrived in the Monte Vista Valley with his father, Farmer, in the early 1800s to cut timber to satisfy Los Angeles's thirst for wood. The cleared land, fertile from dirt washed down the canyon, invited settlement. The Johnsons decided to homestead about 200 acres in Big Tujunga Canyon, part of the San Gabriel Timber Reserve, later to become the Angeles National Forest.[6] Farmer built a small house and sent for his wife and other children, six in all.

As original settlers, the family enjoyed complete

freedom in the canyon. On their ranch, the Johnsons planted vineyards and orchards and kept bees to harvest the honey. In order to irrigate the fruit trees, they dug mile-long ditches along the side of the mountain to divert water from the river. For the hot, dry summers, they built a reservoir.

On the flatter land below, a few other families had also settled in. The Ardizzones and McVines grew grapes; the Bernhardts, grapes and fruit trees; the Adams, olives and peaches; the Wrights, olives; and the Rowleys, fruit. Soon, the Rowleys[7] would open the first general store, and Cornelius's brother John would transform an old hunting lodge into the Monte Vista Inn.[8]

The Johnson's second home on the mesa circa 1912.
Photo courtesy of Glen M. Johnson.

But Farmer's wanderlust prevented him from settling anywhere for too long. After a few years of farming, he decided once again to move on. He sold his land to his sons, Cornelius and John. In his late thirties, Cornelius still lived in the small house built by his father. He seemed content living a simply country life until he met Alice Lee Roybar[9] at the general store.

After losing both her parents to tuberculosis, Alice hoped to find a cure for her own TB. The sixteen-year-old left Iowa and came to live with her great-aunt in the dry, sunny air of Sunland. Her aunt, postmistress Mrs. George Huse, doubled as a correspondent for a Glendale newspaper. She gathered news for her column by reading

The Johnson home many years later as it changed to meet the family's needs.
Photo courtesy of Bolton Hall Museum.

the postcards that came and went in the mail. Alice began studying nursing in Los Angeles, but the physical demands of the job proved too much for her health. Instead, she married the 40-year-old Cornelius in 1908 and went to live in the little house on the slanted mesa. The next year their first daughter, Lucille, arrived.

Three years later Cornelius obtained water rights for the springs up in the mountains. He constructed a pipe system from the springs to irrigate the orchards and to carry water to a new house. With the help of a carpenter, Cornelius built a big, square house further up on the mesa.

Alice's new home included a front room, a dining room, a kitchen with running water, and two bedrooms. The roof extended over a back porch large enough to accommodate a table and chairs. Another little room housed the bath, although toilet facilities remained outside. Instead of the usual galvanized tub with a washboard or wringer, Alice's washing machine operated with a motor turned by water pressure. Electric power in the canyon was years in the future.

Little Lucille helped her father cut wood for the fireplace which kept them warm in winter. In summer, they used a coal oil stove, and coal oil lamps dispensed light. Once a week, her parents shopped in town for groceries; otherwise, they depended on the 'home' orchard of figs, apples, peaches, pomegranates, and oranges for fresh fruit. Cornelius took the grapes from the family's vineyards to Los Angeles markets by horse and buggy, a two-day trip. By 1914, a Buick truck allowed him to drive down to L.A. in the morning and come back the same day. Improved transportation also enabled the family to take a bus and shop in L.A. for clothes.

Like other farm children, Lucille kept busy with chores, especially tending to the chickens. Since no other families lived in the canyon, Lucille had no playmates. She turned to nature for her entertainment and pleasure, thus learning about the flowers and trees and birds. The canyon abounded with wildlife: deer, coyotes, raccoons, skunks,

School picnic in the canyon, June 1910. Photo courtesy of Marshall Murray.

bobcats, ground squirrels, rabbit, snakes, and an occasional mountain lion. But the rattlesnake claimed most of Lucille's attention since it was the most dangerous; other animals tended to be afraid of man and ran away.

Too many encounters, and too many narrow escapes, forced Lucille to learn to deal with the rattlesnakes. She noticed that a rattlesnake can strike only about half its body length, so when the snake stretched out, it was easier

Summertime 1909. Photo courtesy of Marshall Murray.

to kill. A good hard whack with a pitchfork, hoe, gun barrel, shovel, or just a good strong stick, anything sturdy and handy, broke the snake's back and disabled it. The coiled snake was far more dangerous.

Lucille's lonely days ended with the birth of her sister and playmate, Marion, in 1914. They shared many a happy hour with their large collection of dolls. The girls 'sewed' clothes for them by slipping sticks through young, tender alder leaves. Sometimes, they hiked to the river to catch minnows and polliwogs, or they explored the ranch side by side on their horses.

Like all kids, the girls had a mischievous side. When their mother became ill, Cornelius bought some goats, believing the milk would help Alice. When the girls took the goats to the river, they sometimes wandered off, and the girls hid in the brush. Unable to see the girls, the goats panicked and ran for home. Knowing they'd get into trouble because running with bags of milk wasn't good for the goats, the girls hurried to catch up with the goats before they reached home.

When Lucille started school in Sunland's one-room schoolhouse, she walked five miles round-trip each day. By the time she reached fourth grade and Marion was in primary, the school had expanded to two rooms: one teacher for grades one through four, and another teacher for grades five through eight. In the schoolyard, all the children, male and female, played together. The younger children liked to play Indians; the older ones favored baseball, hopscotch, and jacks. At lunch they sometimes hiked down to the wash. The children loved the lavish holiday celebrations at school, especially Halloween, and performing in plays and musicals.

Alice died when Lucille was 12 and Marion 7. The death of a mother is a blow to any child, but in context of the family's isolation in the canyon and the demands of running a ranch, the family missed her all the more. Lucille stepped in to help her father.

Lucille attended Glendale High School for two years. After the City of L.A. annexed Sunland in 1926, Lucille had to transfer to the city high school in San Fernando where she studied economics, cooking, and sewing. High school meant long days; Lucille left home at 6:30 a.m. to catch a bus and didn't get back until 4:00 or 5:00 p.m. Marion missed her sister, her friend and companion, on those long days. While Lucille had spent the early years of her childhood without a playmate, Marion had always had her big sister.

Because of the distance and travel time, few Sunland students participated in extra-curricular activities at the high school. They relied on local activities to socialize. Teens did not date as couples; they planned group activities, often through the church, or went to parties or on hikes. Sometimes they went boating at Lancasters Lake, to dances, or to the movie house in Tujunga.

To avoid the long commute to San Fernando High during her last year, Lucille attended Glendale High. She lived in Glendale by working for room and board and a small salary and only came home on weekends.

After graduation, the girls from the canyon followed

The 1982 flood washed out the road across the canyon, stranding the residents of Riverwood Ranch. Photo courtesy of Bolton Hall Museum.

different paths. Lucille stayed home, caring for the house and doing chores around the ranch, as she'd done for years. One day she called a plumber to repair a problem and met her future husband, Albert Fletcher, whom she married in 1929. Marion returned to the ranch until she met her husband at the Sunland Baptist Church. They married in 1933. Unlike Lucille, Marion worked at jobs outside the home most of her life.

During World War II, Lockheed constantly needed workers to keep pace with their growth spurt. With so many men at war, the plant hired women to fill the jobs. When Marion had worked at the Adams Olive Cannery, men did certain jobs, women did others. For the first time, Marion worked side by side with men at the same job. Because of the women, the company put restrictions on the men's behavior, such as forbidding swearing.

With the sexes thrown together, both doing the same work, Marion witnessed the birth of the "equal work—equal pay" struggle as women grasped the unfairness of their lower pay scale. Later, at Rocketdyne, she discovered a different version of the same problem. The company paid employees according to their classification—and always gave women a different classification than the men. For the same amount of work, for the same skilled labor, the lower classification meant lower wages.

Marion credited the growth of local trailer parks to the

growth of Lockheed during the war years. So many jobs opened that the company also hired from out of state. Local housing could not handle the influx of new people, and trailer parks opened as alternative housing.

Lucille and Marion loved the canyon of their youth: a place of natural beauty crowded with trees and flowers, a running river feeding groves and orchards, wild animals scampering through the brush. The earthquake of February 9, 1971, completely destroyed their childhood home, where Lucille and Albert still lived. The house had been built over a full basement. During the earthquake, the cement foundation crumbled and the whole house slid into the basement, shattering dishes and overturning furniture. When the shaking stopped, the roof was only a foot and a half above the ground. The chimney also collapsed, but not one window broke when the house fell to its doom. Fortunately, no one was hurt, and they later removed their possessions through a window.

Perhaps the destruction of the house paralleled the fate of the canyon. For over a century, man cut down trees, caused fires, and hunted away the wildlife without concern. In the 1900s, Mother Earth answered man's exploitation of the watershed with water shortages in summer and floods in winter. Boulders and sand washed down mountainsides once dense with trees and filled with nature's bounty.

Big Tujunga Canyon with snowcapped mountains.
Both Big Tujunga Canyon and Little Tujunga Canyon were popular
destinations for pleasure trips and for hunting parties,
whether for sport or for food.
Photo courtesy of Bolton Hall Museum.

It really does snow occasionally in Southern California.
Looking north on Eldora after the storm in January 1949.
Photo courtesy of Marshall Murray.

Half a Century Later

The Great Depression dislodged many families who searched for a new beginning. Nobe and Zelda Webber joined the migratory flow when they packed up their belongings and their two-year-old son Larry and left Utah in 1939. They headed south for Los Angeles, in hopes a larger city would offer them better opportunity. Initially, they landed in Glendale where the city rented spaces with stoves in the park. While there, they learned via the grapevine that Dr. Oatey, a Glendale osteopath, needed someone to take care of his ranch in Big Tujunga Canyon.

After some initial discussion, the doctor drove up to their space in the park one day and asked how long it would take them to pack. Zelda replied, "Ten minutes," and quickly gathered up the family's meager belongings. They piled into the doctor's car and headed for Sunland and the canyon.

Up Oro Vista, two miles north of town, they crossed Big Tujunga River. There, nestled in a little valley between two hills, they found their new home. A creek meandered among the ranch buildings: a cabin for them, one the doctor used as a weekend retreat, plus a couple of storage sheds.

Fortunately, Zelda was no stranger to hard work. At age 15, after her father died of cancer, she quit school and went to work in a milk-canning factory to support her mother and six-year-old twin sisters. She'd need her stamina living in a canyon that offered as few amenities in 1939 as it did to the Johnsons half a century earlier. In return for their room and board, the Webbers' duties included taking care of their house and the doctor's, preparing meals for him and his guests, and taking care of the ranch.

Electricity was still a stranger in the canyon; pumps or tanks of gas generated energy. Anyone living in the canyon knew to be prepared. The primitive roads still meandered back and forth across the river. When it rained, the river rose, blocking access to the other side and stranding everyone for days on end. Without telephones to call for help, neighbors relied on each other.

On Saturdays, Dr. Oatey generally brought groceries from the list Zelda had made the week before, although much of what they ate came from the ranch itself. Zelda often served chicken or rabbit for dinner, sometimes turkey or squabs, all garnished with dressing. From the berry patches, she made jam and pies. Favorites were pumpkin, apple, or boysenberry. She also made cakes, especially banana, fudge, ice cream, and root beer soda. When the doctor came to the ranch alone, he usually ate with the Webbers. If he brought guests, Zelda served them in the doctor's cabin.

Larry Webber. If you lived in the canyon, you learned to ride a horse.
Photo courtesy of Zelda Webber.

Any additional

needs, whether groceries or mail or a newspaper, meant saddling the horse for a trip to the general store on Oro Vista and Fenwick, or to the Shopping Bag on Foothill Boulevard. When Larry started kindergarten at Sunland School, Zelda usually took him on horseback too.

A trip to town might actually have offered a welcome relief from the constant rounds of housework: sweeping, dusting, picking-up, cooking, and the inevitable dishes. Piles of clothes always wanted to be washed or ironed or patched. Once Zelda's cabin sparkled, then it was time to turn her attention to the doctor's. And, of course, the once-in-a-while jobs waited: beating rugs, mopping and scrubbing and waxing floors, washing curtains and windows, or varnishing furniture.

If the cabins didn't call for attention, then the outside did. Late fall and winter months focused on cleaning, construction, and repairs. While Nobe handled most of the heavier work, Zelda and Larry pitched in to help. Nobe might dig post holes, set the posts, stretch the wire for fencing around the animal corrals, gardens or along the road, but when he finally put the gate in place, Zelda and Larry picked up the paint cans to finish it.

Brush needed to be cleared, hauled to a safe spot, and burned. Rains always showered the ground with more than moisture. Wood that washed down the mountain had to be cleared out of the way. Rain also washed dirt and sand into the spring. Nobe tried covering it with a screen and putting protective rocks around it, but nothing completely alleviated the necessity of cleaning it. Nobe patched roofs and fixed leaks in the water pipes.

The Angeles National Golf Club, built at the mouth of the wash in 2004, lost two greens to floods a year later.

April showers may bring May flowers, but only with lots of assistance. Nobe rolled up his sleeves to plow and fertilize the fields for sunflowers, kale, corn, and alfalfa. He broke up the hardened ground around the fruit trees and boysenberry patches to aerate the soil. Zelda planted sweet peas, poppies, and tomatoes in the garden he prepared for her. The whole family hiked up the hill to cut hay, which they brought back to the barn for storage.

New or repaired fences protected the plants from ranch animals, but not the wilder creatures looking for food. They shot birds stealing berries or poisoned or trapped squirrels. Rabbit hunting supplied meat for dinner. The rattlesnakes they killed to protect themselves.

The surplus of water in winter became a shortage during summer. The orchards, gardens, and berry patches needed to be watered and weeded. Harvesting and preserving filled the days in late summer and fall. Tending to the animals—goats, calves, rabbits, chickens, turkeys, and horses—was a year-round activity. Besides the essentials like feeding them or milking the goats, Nobe built pens and sheds with cement floors. These required cleaning and spraying several times a year. Fences kept most of the animals safely in corrals, except for the horses, who managed to wander off from time to time. When that happened, the family stopped all other activity to go searching for them. For the winter, Zelda made blankets for the horses; in the summer, Nobe created a shaded area outside the hot barn.

Of course, life was not all work. The Webbers enjoyed horseback riding on secluded trails, surrounded by the natural beauty of the canyon wilderness. Friends came to visit and stayed for dinner or a card game, usually pinochle, or they reciprocated the visits. They danced to the wind-up phonograph or played games like Chinese checkers. Sometimes they went to town to listen to fights, football games, or the World Series on the radio, or to watch a live baseball game in Sunland Park. Larry preferred playing on the swings. From Sunland, they caught a bus to the movies in either Tujunga or Glendale, to watch the popular Shirley Temple or other stars on

Larry and his dog with debris from the storm.
Photo courtesy of Zelda Webber.

the big screen.

On their days off, about one per month, time permitted car trips to Hollywood, Santa Monica, and other points of interest in Los Angeles. January brought the Rose Parade and its fabulous floats, which remain on display after the parade for those who want a closer look. For these simple pleasures, and the security of home and good nourishment, they exchanged all their hard work on the ranch. For the year 1939, they received a total of $85 in cash for services rendered. It was not the labor, but the tragedies to come, that would change their desire to continue living in the canyon.

On January 7, 1940, a roar from the canyon awoke Nobe. He rose to investigate, but could see nothing through the dark curtain of night and the driving rain. The continuing clamor was enough to tell him all was not well, so he awoke Zelda. Grabbing Larry, they ran out of the house and up the hill in their nightclothes. They reached safety just as a wall of water crashed down the canyon.

Huddled together for warmth against the cold night air, they waited until daylight to return to the house. The swollen river had followed the creek down the mountain and washed away everything in its path. Gone was the shed closest to the creek that was used to store the doctor's furniture. Gone was the wood pile for the fireplace. Gone were the animal pens and corrals, although the cows, horses, and goats had managed to escape and survive. In only a few hours, nature asserted its dominance over man's attempts to contain it. Boulders, mud, and debris replaced a year's worth of labor building, repairing, and cleaning.

The storm totally stranded the Webbers. Rocks and boulders so completely blocked the roads that it would take the county weeks to build a new one. Large, rolling waves swept down the river, negating any thought of crossing it. Water; water everywhere—except where they needed it. The storm cut off their water supply, so they were forced to collect rain water for drinking until the river became passable and they could buy it in town. Finally, they managed to reach neighbors and notify Dr. Oatey who left a patient on the table, grabbed his hat, and headed for the ranch. Before they could even consider rebuilding, they faced the mud—everywhere, covering everything.

Only two months later, around noon on March 25, 1940, Larry fell while playing with his dog and slashed his hand between the thumb and finger. While Zelda wrapped his hand in a towel, Nobe hooked the horse to the cart, and they drove to Sunland where they waited for the Glendale bus to get to a doctor. The driver of a passing car saw their obvious distress, stopped, and offered them a ride.

When Dr. Oatey saw Larry's hand, he immediately

took him to a specialist. So horrific was the wound, that the surgeon required the parents to sign a form releasing him from liability if Larry lost use of his thumb. The parents waited fearfully through the long afternoon hours. After darkness fell, Larry woke up. He hand remained bandaged for a long time, while his parents awaited the outcome. When Dr. Oatey finally took the stitches out during a trip to the ranch, everyone breathed a sigh of relief. His thumb not only worked, but it worked well enough not to interfere with his future success as a dentist.

The Tujunga Wash during the dry season.

After the scare from lack of emergency medical services and the traumatic experience with the flood, Zelda refused to live through another year in the canyon. The Webbers stayed over the summer until the rains started, but on October 2, 1940, they moved to Glendale, where Zelda and Nobe gave Larry a brother, Terry, and a sister, Sally. Nobe died five years after their move at age 39 from appendicitis. Left with three children, two of them babies, Zelda searched for employment. She decided on housework, because she could set her own hours and be

The wash during the 1938 flood.
Photo courtesy of Bolton Hall Museum.

home when the kids returned from school. Like his brother Larry, Terry became a dentist and opened a practice in Montrose.

#####

Footnotes

[1] See *Hotels of the Hopeful*, Volume 1 of *The Early History of Sunland, California*.

[2] Sources vary as to whether this was late October or early November.

[3] *The Record-Ledger*, Historical & Progress Edition, May 21, 1953.

[4] "Was Tujunga Bear Country?" *The Leader*, October 31, 1984.

[5] Cornelius Johnson: born October 18, 1867 – died November 4, 1941.

[6] When the San Gabriel Timber Reserve became the Angeles National Forest in 1892, homesteading was no longer allowed.

[7] See *From Crackers to Coal Oil*, Volume 4 of *The Early History of Sunland, California*.

[8] See *Hotels of the Hopeful*, Volume 1 of *The Early History of Sunland, California*.

[9] Alice Lee Roybar: years approximated at 1892 to 1921.

Bibliography

"$1000 Shot." *The Record-Ledger*, Historical & Progress Edition, May 21, 1953.

"Boulevard Only Route to Los Angeles for Early Settlers." *The Record-Ledger*, October 5, 1961.

Cornelius B. Johnson. Funeral record. Bade Mortuary, Tujunga, CA. November 4, 1941.

"Earthquake Ruins Home of Early Local Settler." *The Record-Ledger*, September 27, 1971.

Hitt, Marlene. "Early Settlers Witnessed Some Cataclysmic Changes." *The Foothill Leader*, May 29-30, 1999.

Hitt, Marlene. "Tujunga Settler Shot the Last Grizzly Bear." *The Foothill Leader*, August 21-22, 1999.

Lombard, Sarah. "Mining and Water Claims Embedded in History." *The Record-Ledger*, September 29, 1977.

Lombard, Sarah. "Tujunga Wash—Wilderness Close at Hand." *The Record-Ledger*, October 6, 1977.

"Lucille and Marion Johnson: Two Women from the Canyon." Oral history recorded by Julia Stein. Bolton Hall Museum.

"Old Days on the Big Tujunga." *Trails Magazine*: Vol. 5, No. 1. Winter, 1938.

"Paul Johnson, Born in Big Tujunga Canyon in 1900, Dies at 53." *The Record-Ledger*, December 10, 1953.

Robinson, John W. *The San Gabriels.* Arcadia, CA: Big Santa Anita Historical Society, 1991.

"Saga of Monte Vista." *The Record-Ledger*, Thursday, June 18, 1864.

Tiernan, Mary Lee. *From Crackers to Coal Oil.* Sunland, CA: Snoops Desktop Publishing, 1999.

Tiernan, Mary Lee. *Hotels for the Hopeful.* Sunland, CA: Snoops Desktop Publishing, 1999.

"Was Tujunga Bear Country?" *The Leader*, October 31, 1984.

Webber, Zelda. Personal diary: 1939-1943.

Webber, Zelda. Person interview by Mary Lee Tiernan. July 16, 1999.

The Early History of Sunland, California

8 Volume Series
Also available as ebooks

Vol. 1 *Hotels for the Hopeful* Land promoters of the 1880s promised a perfect life of health, wealth, and pleasure. Although their promises fell short of reality, the village did grow and prosper in the hands of farmers.

Vol. 2 *The Roscoe Robbers and the Sensational Train Robbery of 1894* Two robbers posed as passengers to flag down the train. When the engineer recognized danger, he opened the throttle and sped past. The bandits threw the spur switch, and the train careened full speed off the tracks.

Vol. 3 *The Parson and His Cemetery* Parson Wornum was so loved that when he died, the whole village attended his funeral. Years of neglect of his cemetery spelled disaster in 1978 when heavy rains tore open graves and washed bodies down the hillside.

Vol. 4 *From Crackers to Coal Oil* When a student pulled out his gun and laid it on his desk, the tiny one-room school found itself needing a new teacher. That brought Virginia Newcomb, a romance, and a new family that helped to develop the town, leaving behind a detailed account of pioneer life in a small village.

Vol. 5 *He Never Came Home* Joe Ardizzone, a local grape-grower, doubled as a hit-man for the Mafia. During Prohibition, Joe's bootlegging activities caught him in the middle of in-house quarreling. In 1931, he left on a short trip and disappeared into the pages of history.

Vol. 6 *Lancasters Lake* When Edgar Lancaster dredged the swamp on his land, he created a lake which became a treasured landmark. For 25 years, visitors flocked to its cool shores, and Hollywood used the lake as a set location for some of its early movies.

Vol. 7 *Living in Big Tujunga Canyon* Early settlers, like the Johnson family, found their way into the canyon, a dense woodland bristling with wildlife. 50 years later, the Webber family faced the wrath of the river now winding down a denuded mountainside.

Vol. 8 *From Whence They Came* The Land Boom of the 1880s brought immigrants from around the world. Two generations of Blumfields survived the difficulties of farming and water shortages through industry and imagination.

www.ingramcontent.com/pod-product-compliance
Lightning Source LLC
Chambersburg PA
CBHW061347040426
42444CB00011B/3128